Usborne Naturetrail

Rocks & Fossils

These are crystals of a
mineral called quartz, which
is found in many rocks.

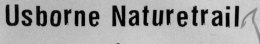

Usborne Naturetrail

Rocks & Fossils

Struan Reid

Designed by
Michael Hill and Kate Rimmer

Illustrated by
Brin Edwards, Non Figg
and Ian Jackson

Edited by Jane Chisholm and Susanna Davidson

Consultant: Professor Dorrik Stow,
University of Southampton National Oceanography Centre

Usborne Quicklinks

The Usborne Quicklinks Website is packed with thousands of links to all the best websites on the internet. The websites include information, video clips, sounds, games and animations that support and enhance the information in Usborne Internet-linked books.

To visit the recommended websites for Naturetrail Rocks & Fossils, go to the Usborne Quicklinks Website at **www.usborne-quicklinks.com** and enter the keywords: **naturetrail rocks**.

When using the internet please follow the internet safety guidelines displayed on the Usborne Quicklinks Website.

The recommended websites in Usborne Quicklinks are regularly reviewed and updated, but Usborne Publishing Ltd. is not responsible for the content or availability of any website other than its own. We recommend that children are supervised while using the internet.

This fish died as it was eating another fish, and then both were fossilized.

CONTENTS

Rock spotting

The restless Earth

Rocks

Minerals

Fossils

Rock collecting

These granite and quartz
pebbles have been tumbled and
washed into shape by the sea.

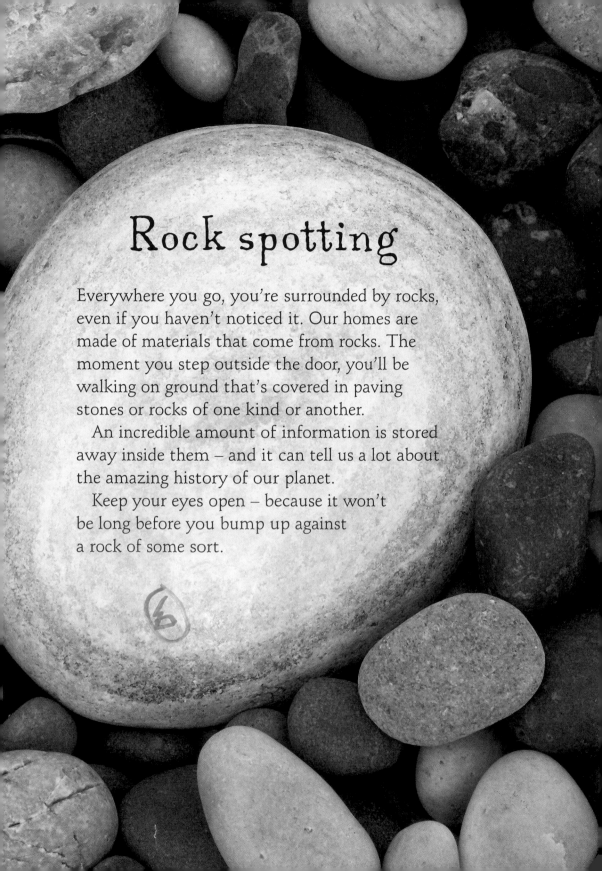

Rock spotting

Everywhere you go, you're surrounded by rocks,
even if you haven't noticed it. Our homes are
made of materials that come from rocks. The
moment you step outside the door, you'll be
walking on ground that's covered in paving
stones or rocks of one kind or another.

An incredible amount of information is stored
away inside them – and it can tell us a lot about
the amazing history of our planet.

Keep your eyes open – because it won't
be long before you bump up against
a rock of some sort.

Rocks, rocks everywhere

Our Earth is made up of rocks and minerals.
You can see them all around you – on mountain
tops and in cliff faces, in deep valleys, riverbeds
and on beaches. Even the homes we live in
are made from stone and building materials,
such as bricks, cement and glass, which are all
created from rocks and minerals.

A delicate shell

Our planet is divided up into three main parts:
a thin, shell-like surface called the crust, then
a layer of solid and hot liquid rock called the
mantle, and a boiling hot bit in the middle
called the core.

The closer to the core of the Earth, the
hotter it gets. These boiling hot layers
sometimes burst out as volcanoes,
shooting molten (melted) rock, ash
and gases into the air.

The mantle is made up
of white-hot rock, about
2,900km (1,800 miles) thick.

Outer core

Inner core

The core consists of an
outer part of molten metal,
and a solid metal inner core.

The Earth's surface or crust
is a thin, rocky shell, just
5-70km (3-43 miles) thick.

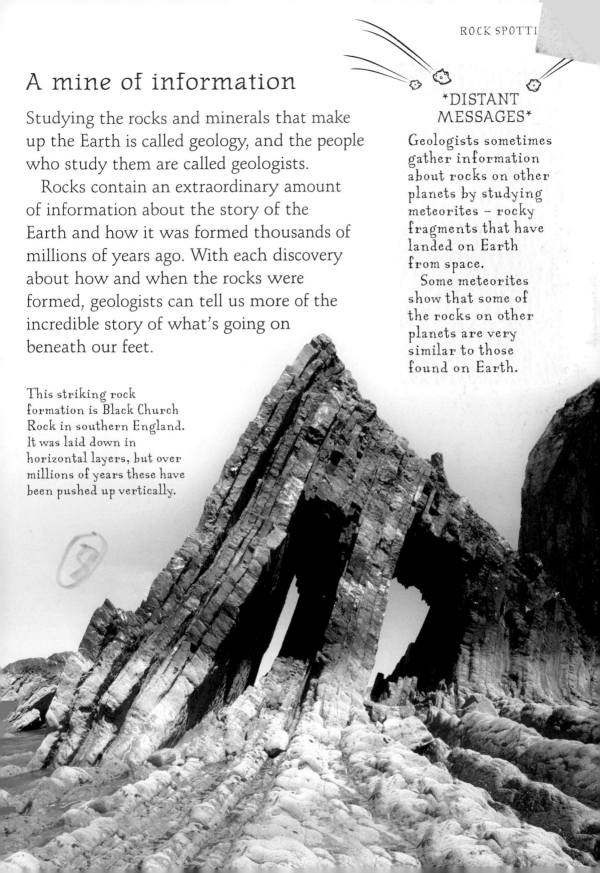

A mine of information

Studying the rocks and minerals that make up the Earth is called geology, and the people who study them are called geologists.

Rocks contain an extraordinary amount of information about the story of the Earth and how it was formed thousands of millions of years ago. With each discovery about how and when the rocks were formed, geologists can tell us more of the incredible story of what's going on beneath our feet.

DISTANT MESSAGES

Geologists sometimes gather information about rocks on other planets by studying meteorites – rocky fragments that have landed on Earth from space.

Some meteorites show that some of the rocks on other planets are very similar to those found on Earth.

This striking rock formation is Black Church Rock in southern England. It was laid down in horizontal layers, but over millions of years these have been pushed up vertically.

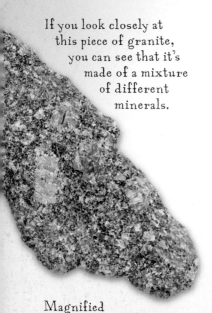

If you look closely at this piece of granite, you can see that it's made of a mixture of different minerals.

Magnified view of granite

Quartz

Dark mica

Pink feldspar

Rocks or minerals?

Minerals are the building blocks that rocks are made of. They consist of simple chemical substances called elements. Some minerals, such as gold and diamond, contain just a single element, but most minerals are combinations of two or more elements.

 Rocks are solid mixtures of minerals – two, three or more of them. If you look very closely at a rock, you can sometimes see the different minerals inside it.

 Geologists divide rocks into three main types, according to the way they were formed. (You can find out more about this on pages 30-41.)

Types of rock	Example
Igneous rock Forms when hot molten rock, known as magma, seeps up from the Earth's mantle and then cools and hardens.	Pegmatite
Sedimentary rock Made from tiny fragments of rock or other materials, called sediment, laid down in layers in lakes, rivers and the sea.	Sandstone
Metamorphic rock A rock that has been changed into a new type of rock by heat or pressure, or sometimes both of these together.	Garnet schist

Soft and wet

You might think of rocks
as being hard, but in fact
they come in different forms.
Soft clay and sand are rocks
too. Some rocks are even created
by the slow dripping of water over
millions of years. These form hanging
spikes known as stalactites, or dripstones.

Stalactites like these
grow about 2cm (1in)
every 120 years.

What are fossils?

Fossils are the preserved remains of animals
and plants that lived thousands or millions
of years ago. A fossil forms when a dead
plant or animal is buried under sediment,
which turns to sedimentary rock. The
remains decay, and the space is
usually filled with
minerals.

Sometimes hard
parts such as shells
survive — as you
can see in this
fossil of a turtle.

HOW FOSSILS ARE MADE

Fossils are created
when sediment, such
as sand or mud, is
washed or blown over
the remains of plants
or animals. As they
rot away, the space
fills with minerals
from the sediment
and from water.

Fossilization takes
place by pure chance,
only if the remains
are buried quickly.

Looking for rocks

You don't need a lot of equipment on a
rock-spotting trip, but a few simple things
will be very useful to carry with you.

Map in hand

One of the most important things to take is a
good map of the area, so you know where to
look. It should show the shape of the land and
the main rock outcrops to be seen, as well as
any towns, roads and paths.

Here is a very simple illustration of some of the
features you should find on your map.

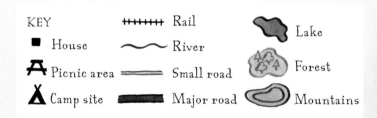

KEY

- House
- Picnic area
- Camp site

Rail
River
Small road
Major road

Lake
Forest
Mountains

12

Choosing a field guide

Before choosing a guide, make sure it covers the range of rocks you are likely to see in your area. It should be divided into sections on minerals, rocks and fossils. For example, can you find these fossils in the guide below?

Compare these fossils to the ones in your guide. Do they have the same patterns on them?

Echinoid fossils

INSIDE YOUR GUIDE

*Your guide should show the rocks divided into three groups: igneous, sedimentary and metamorphic.

*Minerals should be divided into three main groups: rock-forming, ore minerals and gemstones.

*Fossils should be grouped according to whether they're fish, animals or plants.

*Your guide should contain clear, bite-sized facts and good pictures for easy checking.

1. Flip through the guide. Is your example easy to find?

2. What are the illustrations like? Is it easy to recognize your rock or fossil example?

3. Are the words clear and easy to read?

4. Does the description tell you all you want to know?

Fossils

➡ Gastropods
These are commonly known as snails. Their shells are usually coiled in spirals. Their fossils are found in shales, mudstones and limestones formed as far back as 540 million years ago.

Three different kinds of gastropods

➡ Bivalves
These include cockles, mussels and razor shells. Their shells are made of two separate parts, called valves, that are hinged together so the animals inside can open them up to feed and close them for protection. Their fossils are found in shales, limestones and mudstones.

Two different bivalves

➡ Brachiopods
Like bivalves, brachiopods have a hinged pair of shells, but the two are a different size and shape, so that one overlaps the other. Their fossils are found in shales, limestones and mudstones, especially those formed between 500 and 285 million years ago.

Some brachiopods' shells have grooves and ridges.

➡ Echinoids (sea urchins)
These are rounded or heart-shaped animals up to 100mm (4in) across. The shell is made of plates of calcite, often covered with lumps. On modern-day sea urchins spines are attached to these lumps, but the spines are rarely preserved in fossils. Echinoids are found in rocks, especially chalk, that were formed less than 200 million years ago.

Echinoid fossil with lumps, showing where the spines used to be

Heart-shaped echinoid fossil

A modern-day sea urchin with spines

56

TOP TIPS

The shapes of hills, the patterns of rivers, and the types of soil all hold clues about what kinds of rocks there are beneath your feet. Trees and plants can also give clues about the types of rocks that lie under them.

A walk in the country

One of the most enjoyable ways to spot rocks is to go for a walk in the countryside. You don't have to go very far before you'll find yourself surrounded by many kinds of rocks and minerals.

Although much of the landscape may be covered by grass and trees, you'll still find rocks peeking out in exposed places.

Over thousands of years, a river cuts through the rocky landscape, leaving rocks and stones in its banks.

Stone walls built around fields are a useful clue to what type of rock there is in the area.

A waterfall forms if hard rock stops the water from making a deeper channel.

Mountainous areas usually have lots of rocks. The soil is thinner in these places, as it has been gradually washed away by rain.

Moss and lichen

The foot of a cliff is a good place to look for rock fragments and fossils.

Granite is a common rock. Sometimes you'll find huge granite boulders stacked up on top of each other.

Good areas to look are hills and mountains, cliffs and riverbanks, as these are places where it's common to find bare patches of rock. You may come across piles of rocks at the bottom of cliffs too.

WORN AWAY

Granite boulders are the remains of hard igneous rock that has been pushed up under mountains made of a softer rock.

When the mountains have been worn away by wind and rain, the granite is left standing on its own.

Soft rock worn away

Beachcombing

Beaches are good places to study all kinds of rocks, minerals and fossils. Some beaches have a mixture of rocks and sand on them, while others consist of just pebbles.

If you look closely at a sandy beach, you'll find clues about what types of rock the sand is made of. Pale sand contains limestone fragments, and dark sand is made from black volcanic basalt.

Pebbles

Pebbles are shaped by the sea as it batters rock from cliffs and then rolls the pieces around, making them smooth and round. They're easy to pick up and examine, so you can get a close-up view of the types of rocks and minerals in the area.

Rocky beaches can make perfect little fishing ponds for seabirds to feed from.

Most sand is yellow-brown. The shade comes from glassy quartz covered in iron-oxide (rust).

Layers and fossils

Beach cliffs are often striped with different shades of rock, showing how sedimentary rocks have been laid down in layers over millions of years.

You can sometimes find fossils lying on the beach below. These have been weathered out of the cliff face, especially after winter storms.

STRANGERS ON THE SHORE

Not all the rocks and pebbles on a beach are local to the area. Some may have been carried from far away by rivers or glaciers millions of years ago.

Here you can clearly see the bands in the rocks, showing how they were laid down in layers.

Sea stacks are the remains of ancient cliffs worn away by the sea.

WATCH OUT

*Be careful when walking near cliffs as there may be loose rocks. Look out for any signs warning you to keep away, and never go near edges.

*Check with the local tourist office about tide times, and walk on the beach when the tide is going out.

Boulders from the cliff have been washed smooth by the sea.

Look out for fossils in the rocks beneath a cliff.

Towns and gardens

You could look for many kinds of rocky evidence close to home. By looking at the buildings in your town, you may find out about the types of rocks in your area – and you could make a record of your discoveries.

Write down what you see. You may have to do extra research to find out what everything is made of.

KEY QUESTIONS

1. What's on the path or pavement you're walking on? Is it made of gravel, stone or concrete slabs?

2. Is there any stone edging to the pavement? If so, it may be made of hard granite.

3. Look at the other houses on the street. Are they all made of the same materials?

4. If not, do you think some of the materials may have been brought in from somewhere else?

5. What's on the roof? Roof materials can change – slate or stone in one area, clay tiles in another.

Church could be made from local stone

Viewing and sketching points

Church

Paving slabs

Cobbled road

Looks like slate roof on house

Old building made from local sandstone

Hard stone fountain – granite?

Modern block of flats made of concrete

Town hall with marble pillars

You could make sketches of the buildings and stick them in a notebook.

What's your soil like?

All soil is divided into three main types: acid, alkaline and neutral. The rocks below affect the soil on top. You can find out about the type of soil in your garden or park by measuring its pH (potential of hydrogen) level – this is its acidity or alkalinity.

You can do this with a simple homemade test. You'll need a small sample of soil, a red cabbage and some paper coffee filters.

Red cabbage

1. Slice the red cabbage into small pieces until you have about 2 cups of chopped cabbage.

2. Place the pieces in a saucepan, cover them with water and simmer for 15 minutes. Allow to cool.

Sieve

3. Strain the cold liquid through a sieve into a bowl. It should be a shade of deep red or purple.

Coffee filter paper

4. Soak a filter paper in the liquid. Allow the paper to dry and then cut it into strips about 2cm (1in) wide.

Stir the mixture

5. Place your soil sample in a plastic bowl. Add some water to it and stir it up into a thick soup.

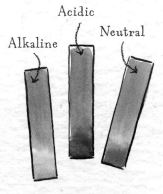

Acidic

Alkaline   Neutral

6. Dip in a paper strip. If it turns green-yellow, the soil is alkaline. If red, acidic. Purple-blue means neutral.

Molten lava pours from a
volcano. This is all part of the
Earth's endless cycle of change.

The restless Earth

The Earth has been changing continuously over millions of years. Sometimes you can see these changes in a dramatic way – when an earthquake splits open the ground, or when a volcano explodes.

But many of the changes take place very, very slowly beneath our feet, unseen and unheard. While up above, on the surface, rocks are being gradually worn and weathered away by wind and water.

GOING AROUND

You can see the same
heating and cooling
process when you heat
a pan of water.

A plume of boiling water
rises up in the middle and
spreads over the surface.

As the water spreads,
it cools and sinks down
again at the edges.

Always be very careful
when experimenting
with hot liquids.

A warm heart

Many of the rocks you see
around you started life deep
inside the Earth, and most
of the others have also been
affected in some way by heat
from the Earth's core.

The core works rather like a
huge engine that generates heat.
The heat travels out from the core
and melts part of the rock in the
mantle, which rises up and spreads
out. As it spreads, it cools and then
sinks back down, and the process
begins all over again.

In this diagram you can see the
continuous cycle taking place
beneath the Earth's surface.

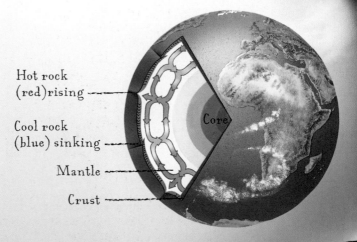

Hot rock
(red) rising

Cool rock
(blue) sinking

Core

Mantle

Crust

Drilling holes

Geologists can only directly
study the surface rocks of the
crust. Below this, they have to
drill holes to collect the rocks.
They can't drill any deeper
than 16km (10 miles), though,
because the heat and pressure
would be too great.

Pumice is one of the
rocks that shoots out of
volcanoes. It is full of
tiny holes made by gases.

Blow-outs

During volcanic eruptions,
intense heat within the crust
and mantle pushes very hot
liquid up, and forces it out
through cracks in the crust.
Boiling rock, thick clouds of
ash and poisonous gases are
shot into the air and scattered
over the surrounding land.

Volcanoes can be extremely
destructive, but they can also
give geologists a chance to
learn a lot more about rocks
deep inside the Earth.

This is Kilauea volcano in
Hawaii, which has been erupting
continuously since 1983.

A NEW ISLAND

There are volcanoes
under the sea, as
well as on land, and
sometimes they can
create new islands
when they erupt. This
happened in 1963
when an eruption off
the coast of Iceland
forced up a new rocky
island named Surtsey.

Our moving world

You might think the Earth's crust would be one solid piece, but it's actually divided into sections, called plates, that fit closely together like parts of a giant jigsaw puzzle. These plates are constantly moving around very slowly, driven along by the heating and cooling process inside the mantle.

The plates often slide, crunch and grind past each other, generating massive friction. Sometimes they push against each other or pull apart. But most of the time we're unaware of any of this.

CRUSTY BITS

The Earth has two types of crust.

Thick crust, called continental crust, forms areas of land, while much thinner crust makes up the floors of the oceans.

Each plate consists of either continental or oceanic crust, or some of both.

Continental crust is 20-70km (12-43 miles) thick.

Oceanic crust is 5-10km (3-6 miles) thick.

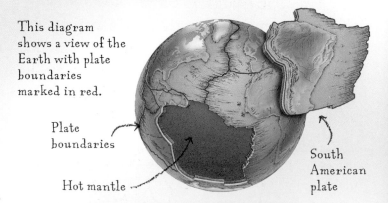

This diagram shows a view of the Earth with plate boundaries marked in red.

Plate boundaries

Hot mantle

South American plate

Mountains and trenches

When two plates in the continental crust push into each other, the crust crumples and folds upward to form fold mountains.

When plates on the ocean floor move apart, magma rises up to fill the gap and sometimes forms underwater mountains called ridges.

When they push against each other, one is forced beneath the other to form a deep trench in the ocean.

The Himalayas in Asia are fold mountains, and the highest mountains in the world.

Great shakes

Plate boundaries are always cracked and jagged. This means that, as they slide past each other, they can lock together, causing a huge amount of energy to build up. Eventually, one plate is forced to give way and great pulses of energy surge out in the form of an earthquake.

Over a million earthquakes occur every year, but we can't even feel most of them.

PUSHING PLATES

When two plates meet head on, one of them has to give way.

On land, one of the plates is forced up and over to form a fold.

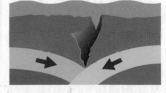

A trench is formed on the ocean floor when one plate is forced down.

Weather and weathering

There is a lot happening on the Earth's surface too. Wind and rain, boiling hot and freezing cold temperatures gradually eat away at the landscape, wearing down and reshaping all the rocks and minerals on the surface. This has been going on ever since the Earth began.

Here are some of the ways it happens.

Frying and freezing

As temperatures rise and fall, rock expands and contracts, making it crack. Rainwater seeps into the cracks, then freezes and expands, shattering the rock.

Weak spots

Some minerals are easily dissolved by water and form weak spots in the rock. If one mineral gives way, others are exposed. Then cracks start to appear and the rock begins to crumble and break up.

Blasted by the wind

Winds full of particles such as sand whip rocky landscapes into shape. This sandblasting wears away the rock surfaces and can form weird and wonderful shapes.

Battered by the sea

*Sea waves can batter rocky headlands, carving out arches. The arches eventually collapse to leave tall sea stacks.

*Weak rocks in the middle of a sea cliff may be worn away by waves to form a cave.

*The rock fragments end up in the sea where they are slowly ground up into sand.

Carried away

*Streams and rivers carry rocks and worn-down fragments toward the sea.

*Slow-moving glaciers creep down mountains, carving out U-shaped valleys and pushing along rocks as they go.

*Rain washes rocky mountain faces smooth.

*In desert areas, gushing water from sudden flash floods can cut deep into soft rocks.

Under the ground

*Weathered and eroded rock is known as sediment and it can build up and harden into layers of sedimentary rock on the ocean floor.

*Where one of the Earth's plates slides beneath another, the sediment is dragged down into the mantle, where it is melted and squeezed. Then the cycle of rock-making begins again.

In this striped sandstone
landscape you can see how
the rock was laid down,
layer upon layer.

Rocks

The Earth is made up from many different rocks, but they can all be divided into one of three types, according to the way they were made.

The most common type is formed by being melted and mixed up in the great bubbling cauldron beneath the Earth's crust. The second type is broken up by wind and water and then laid down in compact layers. The third is created when existing rocks are heated and squeezed so much that they're transformed into new rocks.

Hot rocks

Most rocks are formed when hot, molten
rock, called magma, rises up from the mantle
and then cools and solidifies. The types of
rocks this makes are called igneous rocks.

Intruding rocks

Sometimes, instead of reaching the
surface, magma rises up and forces its way
– or "intrudes" – between other rocks and
hardens inside the Earth's crust. The kind of
rock this makes is called "intrusive" igneous
rock. Some of this rock only emerges on
the surface millions of years later, when the
rocks on top have been weathered away.
A common example is granite.

At Le Puy in France, an intrusive
"plug" of magma hardened inside
a volcano. The surrounding
rock was worn away, leaving
the plug on its own.

The Giant's Causeway in Ireland is made up of columns of extrusive basalt rock that formed as volcanic lava cooled and contracted.

Volcanic rock

The other type of igneous rock is called "extrusive" (meaning "forced out") igneous rock. This forms when the magma, as boiling lava, is forced up through a volcano and onto the Earth's surface, where it cools and hardens. Basalt is a common example.

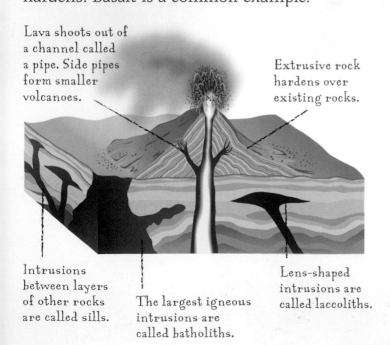

Lava shoots out of a channel called a pipe. Side pipes form smaller volcanoes.

Extrusive rock hardens over existing rocks.

Intrusions between layers of other rocks are called sills.

The largest igneous intrusions are called batholiths.

Lens-shaped intrusions are called laccoliths.

HOT SPRINGS

The great heat from a volcano not only heats up the surrounding ground – but any water in the ground too. The boiling water sometimes shoots out as hot springs.

Steam from the hot water can be used to power electricity turbines, and minerals in the water and mud can be used in health treatments.

Igneous rocks to spot

Igneous rocks make up most of the rocks in
the Earth's crust. So they're the rocks you
will probably find more of when you are out
on a collecting expedition.

Here's a selection of some of the most
common igneous rocks to look out for – both
intrusive and extrusive.

Granite
Common intrusive rock,
ranging from white to
pink. Mottled because
it contains minerals of
mica, quartz and feldspar
which are easy to spot.

Peridotite
Intrusive rock, varying
from fine to coarse.
Ranges from dark to
light green, and often
occurs with metals such
as nickel and platinum.

Agglomerate
Extrusive, made of
large rounded lumps of
volcanic rock such as
basalt. May come from
pieces of volcanic lava
that cooled in the air.

Rhyolite
Extrusive rock, same
composition as granite,
but with finer grains.
Pale or white, but can be
reddish or black. Found
in volcanic pipes.

Pegmatite
A very coarse intrusive rock with large crystals in it. This makes it easy to study its minerals, mostly feldspar, quartz and mica.

Gabbro
Intrusive igneous rock, coarse-grained with a smooth texture. Formed when magma cools slowly. Dark greenish, speckled with minerals.

Obsidian
Extrusive, natural glass formed when volcanic magma cools quickly. Black and splinters to give sharp edges and smooth surfaces.

Pumice
Extrusive volcanic rock full of gas bubbles made when magma cools quickly. Very light so it can float on water. Pale, often used as an abrasive.

Basalt
Fine- to medium-grained dark extrusive volcanic rock. As the lava cools, it may shrink and crack into six-sided columns. Covers large areas.

Tuff
Made from small pieces of volcanic rock and crystals cemented into hard rock. Extrusive, built up in layers of ash from volcanic explosions.

Dolerite
Also called diabase, a medium-grained intrusive rock, ranging from black to green. One of the most common rocks in the Earth's crust.

Andesite
Common extrusive rock, but only found in volcanic areas on land. Fine-grained and glassy. Often speckled pale green, purple, or brown.

Serpentine
Intrusive, an altered form of peridotite. Mainly composed of the mineral serpentine. Usually dark green, but may have red, green and white stripes.

LAYERS OF SEDIMENT

You could try this experiment to see how sediment separates into different layers when mixed in water.

Water → ← Soil mix

Fill a tall glass jar about one-third full with a mixture of soil and gravel, then add some water.

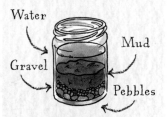

Water → ← Mud

Gravel → ← Pebbles

Stir well and leave it to settle. In a few days you will see "graded bedding" with the heavier material lying at the bottom.

Layered rocks

Rocks formed in layers are known as sedimentary rocks.

Some sedimentary rocks, such as sandstone, are made from fragments of other rocks. Others, such as limestone, are made from animal remains such as shells, or from chemical crystals and volcanic ash. The fragments, or sediments, are laid down in layers at the bottom of seas, rivers and lakes.

Large and heavy fragments settle first, while smaller and lighter pieces settle more slowly.

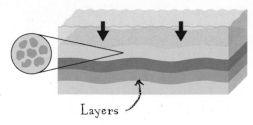

Layers

As new sediments settle on the sea floor, their weight presses down on the layers below, making them more compact.

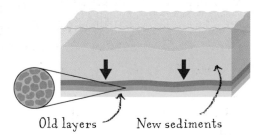

Old layers   New sediments

Limestone landscapes

Limestone is made up mainly of a mineral called calcite, which comes from the shelly remains of tiny sea creatures.

Calcite dissolves easily in rainwater, creating some extraordinary landscapes. Rain eats away at the stone, producing underground caves, towering pinnacles and other amazing shapes.

Limestone

The Grand Canyon

The Grand Canyon in the USA is one of the most spectacular places to see layers of sedimentary rock. It cuts down through nearly 2km (1¼ miles) of sediment to show layers that were laid down over millions of years. The layers range from over 2,000 million years old at the bottom, to about 60 million years old at the top.

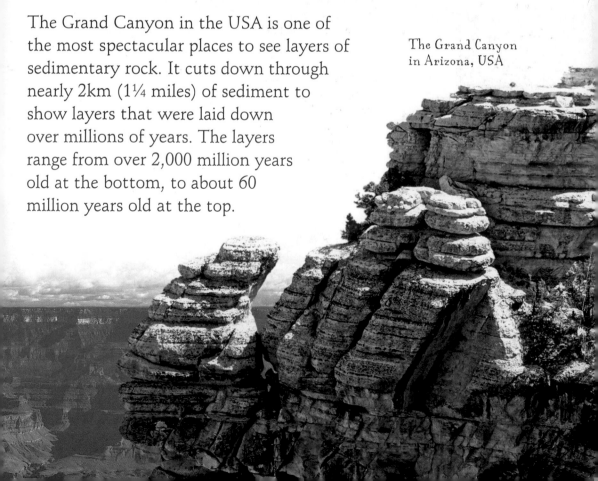

The Grand Canyon in Arizona, USA

FINE CHINA

Although it's soft, clay is actually a type of sedimentary rock. The purest clay of all is called kaolin, or china clay, and it's used to make delicate pieces of pottery.

Sedimentary rocks to spot

Sedimentary rocks consist of fragments of rock, seashells and minerals, mixed up and laid down in layers, on the Earth's surface and under the sea.

They're especially valuable to geologists, because the layers can provide a detailed record of the Earth's history. Sedimentary rocks are also the main source of fossils.

Chalk
A very fine-grained type of limestone. Composed of the skeletons of tiny sea animals. Fossils such as sea urchins are often found in it.

Sandstone
Formed of grains of sand – usually from quartz, feldspar and other mineral or rock fragments – under the sea, in rivers and deserts.

Limestone
A common rock, made up mainly of the mineral calcite from the fossil remains of sea creatures. Usually cream, but can also be dark or reddish.

Uluru or Ayers Rock in Australia is an enormous outcrop of sandstone, and it is sacred to the local Aboriginal people.

Conglomerate
Formed from rounded fragments of rock washed down rivers and along coastlines. Fragments of any size, and often have sandy material between.

Stalactites
Found in limestone areas. They hang from the roofs of caves and are formed by the slow dripping of water containing the mineral calcite.

Mudstone and Shale
Formed from hardened sea mud. If the rock parts easily in fine layers it is called shale; if not, it is called mudstone. Black, brown, red or green.

Breccia
Like conglomerate, made of rock fragments set in sandy material. Fragments are angular, showing they were not carried far by water.

Flint
Dark, glassy rock made of chalcedony. Nodules or round lumps often the size of a potato. They separate easily from surrounding rock. Found in chalk.

Tufa
Formed when the mineral calcite hardens out of water around natural springs or hot springs. Has lots of holes and a spongy appearance.

Coal
Black, soft or hard, formed from fossilized plant remains in bogs or swamps. Found in layers, or seams, between other rocks such as sandstone.

Oolite
A type of limestone, made of tiny ball-shaped grains of calcite called ooliths. Yellow, white, sometimes brown. Shells and other fossils often found in it.

Gypsum
Develops when salty water evaporates. Very common. Uniform, fine-grained gypsum, known as alabaster, is soft and often used for carving.

Contact metamorphic rocks usually form near igneous rocks when hot magma heats up the nearby rocks and changes the minerals inside them.

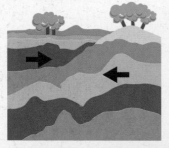

Regional metamorphic rocks are created when the Earth's plates squeeze against each other.

Making new rocks

When igneous or sedimentary rocks are heated and squeezed deep inside the Earth, the minerals inside them are completely changed, forming a new type of rock. This is called metamorphic rock.

This transformation happens in two ways. When rocks are changed by heat alone they're known as "contact" metamorphic rocks.

But when they're changed by great pressure, as well as heat, they're called "regional" metamorphic rocks. Regional metamorphic rocks are the most common of the two types.

Bow Fiddle Sea Stack is an arch of metamorphic quartzite rock on the north east coast of Scotland. It is part of the Caledonian range of fold mountains.

Limestone to marble

One of the best-known metamorphic rocks is marble, which is formed when limestone is heated and squeezed.

If the original limestone is very pure, with no other chemicals in it, the marble will be very white. Impurities produce a marble with stripes of red, yellow, brown, blue or green against a white background.

Quartz into quartzite

Quartzite is a contact metamorphic rock, although it can also be formed by regional metamorphism. It is made from sedimentary sandstone, which consists almost entirely of grains of quartz.

Extreme heat changes the quartz grains into a mass of interlocking crystals, forming quartzite. Quartzite is very hard and you can often see it on exposed hillsides, in riverbanks and road cuttings.

Marble with impurities can produce beautiful decorative building stone.

MARBLE MAHAL

Some of the world's most beautiful buildings, including the Taj Mahal in India and the Parthenon in Athens, are made from marble. Some marble is softer than others and is easily eroded by wind, rain and pollution.

Quartz is the main ingredient of quartzite, sometimes mixed with other minerals such as feldspar and mica.

SQUEEZED OUT

It is very unusual to find any pebbles or fossils inside metamorphic rocks. This is because the heat and pressure involved in making metamorphic rock is so great that the shapes of the pebbles and fossils are either changed or destroyed.

The pebbles in this stone have been squeezed into ovals.

This fossil of a trilobite has been squeezed out of shape.

The Parthenon temple in Athens was built of marble by the Greeks about 2,500 years ago.

Metamorphic rocks to spot

Metamorphic rocks are formed when igneous or sedimentary rocks are changed by heat and pressure, or by heat alone. They are some of the most interesting rocks to look at, because you can often clearly see the mixture of rocks they are made up from, in the form of stripes and swirling patterns. Here are some common examples of metamorphic rocks.

Gneiss
Formed by heat and pressure. Coarse-grained and consists mostly of the minerals feldspar, mica and quartz, arranged in irregular (wavy) bands.

Marble
Mainly made of the mineral calcite. Formed by heat or pressure on limestone. Common, and can be found in mountain areas all over the world.

Mica schist
Schists are fine-grained, layered rocks from mudstone and siltstone. Mica schist contains the mineral mica, making it dark or silvery.

Garnet schist
Similar to mica schist, but also contains garnets. Rounded in shape, varying in size and often dark red, green or white. Splits easily.

Quartzite
Consists mainly of grains of quartz, but can contain feldspar, mica or other minerals. Made of metamorphosed quartz sandstone. Often white.

Amphibolite
A medium- to coarse-grained rock, mostly of hornblende and feldspar. Formed from igneous rocks such as basalt. Dark with pale bands.

Steatite
Also known as soapstone, created by heat and pressure. Largely consists of mineral talc. Slightly slippery to touch, hence its name. Soft, easy to carve.

Phyllite
Formed from shale and mudstone. Created under great heat and pressure. Green, pale or silvery, with a shiny surface. Splits easily.

Slate
Formed when shale and mudstone are heated and squeezed. Consists of tiny grains of minerals such as mica. Black, red, green or purple. Splits easily.

Skarn
Formed from limestone in contact with granite. Found in northern Europe, Japan and USA, it is often a source of iron and copper.

Migmatite
A mixed rock that is part metamorphic and part igneous. The two components occur in very irregular bands. Makes an attractive building stone.

Cement is a building material made from crushed limestone. You can use it to make your own hand prints.

1. Empty a small bag of cement into a bucket. Slowly add water a little at a time, following the instructions on the bag.

2. Stir the mixture each time you add water, until it becomes smooth and firm. Pour it onto a tray with raised edges.

3. Spread it out evenly. Wearing rubber gloves, press your hands onto it. Leave it for a day and your prints will be set hard.

Using rocks

People have been using rocks as materials for building and as tools for making things for hundreds of thousands of years. We've dug and blasted them out of the ground, cut them into pieces and crushed them into powder. And, by doing all this, we've changed the landscape too.

The first tools

One of the very first rocks to be used as a tool was flint. Flint is a hard, glassy stone found in potato-sized lumps called nodules, and it can be chipped to form sharp edges for cutting and piercing. Some of the earliest flint tools found are about 700,000 years old.

Flint was used by early people to make knives, spears, axes and arrowheads. Other rocks, such as granite and limestone, were chipped and shaped into tools such as grinding stones and hammers.

Softer stones, such as marble and alabaster, are much easier to cut and carve. So they were rubbed and polished with sand to make sculptures.

This flint hand axe was made about 250,000 years ago and it would have been used to chop up meat for eating.

Painting with rocks

More than 20,000 years ago, early artists decorated the walls of caves using paints made from crushed rocks, clays, chalk, earth and charcoal with animal fat and water. Some rocks are still used to make paints today.

The caves at Lascaux in France were decorated about 17,000 years ago using paints made from rocks.

PAINT STONES

Here are some stones used to make paints.

Lapis lazuli - blue

Malachite - green

Cinnabar - red

Building stones

The first homes were made of grasses and even animal bones and skins. But once people had the tools to dig and cut rocks, they started using stone instead.

Man-made building materials such as bricks, cement and glass are also made from crushed rocks and minerals.

The Egyptian pyramids were built nearly 5,000 years ago from huge limestone blocks.

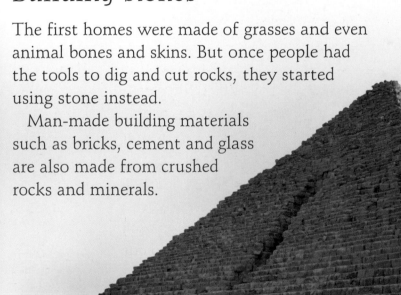

Quartz crystals growing
inside a hollow ball of
rock called a geode

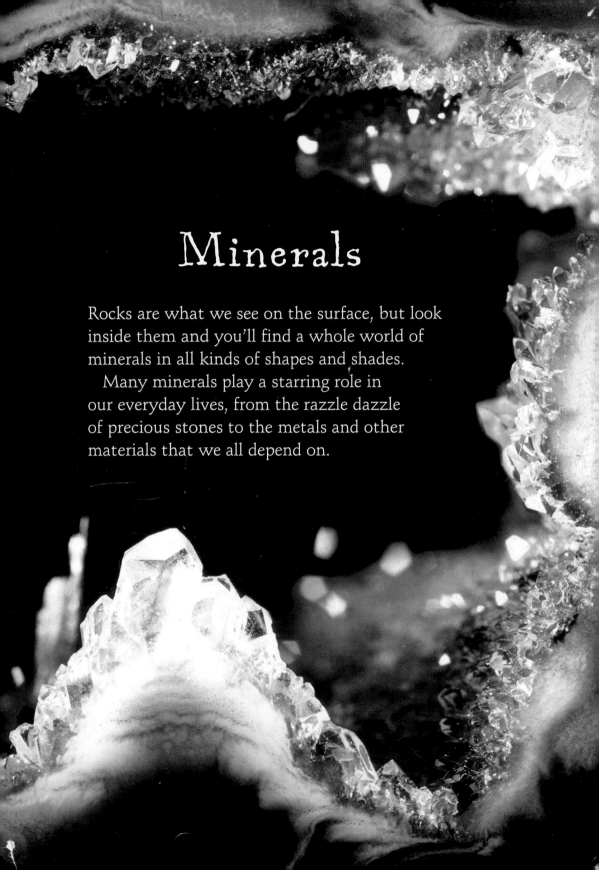

Minerals

Rocks are what we see on the surface, but look inside them and you'll find a whole world of minerals in all kinds of shapes and shades.
Many minerals play a starring role in our everyday lives, from the razzle dazzle of precious stones to the metals and other materials that we all depend on.

Mineral building blocks

Minerals are the building blocks of rocks. Although there are thousands of different minerals, only a few hundred of these are common ingredients in rocks. Some of them are the source of materials we use every day, but many more are very rare and valuable.

Crystal power

Minerals are made up of simple chemical substances called elements, such as oxygen, silicon, iron and calcium. Most of them come in the form of little blocks called crystals, that lock together to form hard, solid rock.

Some of the best crystals are found in hollow balls of rock called geodes. Hot gases or liquids seep in and crystallize as they cool.

You may be lucky enough to find a geode. If you crack it open like an egg, you'll find crystals inside.

Diamonds are sometimes found in a volcanic rock known as kimberlite.

This diamond has been cut and polished. A diamond in its natural state is shown above.

Native elements

Most minerals are made up of two or more elements but a few, like diamond, consist of just one. These are called native elements.

Diamonds grow when the element carbon is heated and squeezed inside the upper mantle of the Earth. They can sometimes be carried to the surface during volcanic eruptions.

Identifying minerals

Most mineral crystals have a regular shape or structure. This gives geologists important clues to help them to identify the minerals in rocks. You can find out more about crystals and their shapes on the next page.

Crystal patterns

One of the things that makes crystals special is that they all come in regular, or symmetrical, shapes. For example, for every side or "face" on a crystal, there is another face on the other side of the crystal that is parallel to it.

This is because the different elements in a mineral always group together in the same proportion. The elements form simple patterns, and the pattern is always the same in any particular mineral. This helps geologists to identify them.

REGULAR SHAPES

Many minerals can be identified by their shapes. If you look closely at a crystal and can count the number of sides, or faces, it has, and at what angle they meet, it'll help you to identify what family it belongs to.

Here are some typical crystal shapes.

Cubic

Monoclinic

Hexagonal

Rhombic

Tetragonal

Triclinic

Even though these quartz crystals are growing in different directions, each one has parallel faces.

Grow your own crystals

You can grow your own crystals, either using a kit from a hobby shop or some table salt from the kitchen. You'll also need a glass jar, some hot water, a pencil, a piece of string, a paperclip and a metal spoon.

HANDY HINT
If you don't have any salt, try using baking soda or sugar instead. To make brighter crystals, you could also add a drop of food dye or ink to the water.

The spoon will protect the jar by preventing the hot water from cracking the glass.

1. Place the spoon in the jar. Then slowly pour in hot water so that it's about three-quarters full.

Some salt will stay at the bottom of the jar.

2. Add the salt slowly and keep stirring until no more will dissolve. This is called a saturated solution.

The string should be long enough so the paperclip can hang in the middle of the jar.

3. Tie the string to the middle of a pencil, and then tie the paperclip to the other end of the string.

4. Lower the paperclip into the jar, resting the pencil on top. Then leave the jar for a couple of days.

5. After a day, you'll see salt crystals forming on the string and the paperclip and at the water surface.

Salt crystals are also called halite crystals. They are found in sedimentary rocks in lumps, or as single cubic crystals.

Making minerals

Many of the Earth's minerals can be found in a whole range of different rocks – igneous, sedimentary and metamorphic. But some minerals are usually only found in just one type of rock.

Minerals in igneous rocks

Many minerals develop directly inside the magma as igneous rocks are forming. Others develop when gases escape from the magma and a reaction takes place with the rock next to it, or as the magma cools.

Minerals created like this are known as igneous minerals. They include some of the more common minerals, such as feldspars, micas and quartz.

Feldspar is one of the main minerals in this volcanic basalt rock.

New minerals

Some new "metamorphic" minerals develop when minerals in rocks go through chemical changes. This happens during the metamorphic process, when the rocks are pulled down into deeper parts of the Earth's crust and heated and squeezed.

Garnet is an example of a metamorphic mineral. It is found in many metamorphic rocks, such as gneisses and schists, and can range from dark red and pink to brown and bright green. The finest garnet crystals are used as gemstones (see page 54).

A bright pink garnet crystal set in quartz and calcite

Other minerals

Some minerals develop when rocks on the Earth's surface are weathered by water and chemicals. Common examples are members of the clay mineral group, such as kaolinite and chlorite. Others, such as calcite which makes up limestone, are formed as the hard parts of animals. Still others, such as gypsum and halite, form as salty water evaporates.

TURQUOISE

Turquoise is a pale blue sedimentary mineral formed when water reacts with rocks that contain aluminium (aluminum). The best turquoise comes from Iran, where it has been mined for over 3,000 years.

Polished turquoise

Turquoise fragment

Gypsum

Calcite

Halite

Rock-forming minerals

There are about 3,500 known minerals, and scientists discover about 20 new ones every year. But only a small number of these make up nearly all of the rocks in the Earth's crust.

The most common minerals of all belong to the huge silicate family. There are about 1,000 different types of silicate, including quartz, which also comes in many different varieties.

Fluorite
Also called fluorspar, forms cube-shaped crystals. Blue, purple, green or yellow. Glows in ultra-violet light, creating fluorescence.

Halite
Also known as rock salt, this is the salt we eat. Transparent or white in its purest form, but usually stained brown or yellow. Tastes salty.

Apatite
Mined from rocks for use as a fertilizer. Your teeth are also made mostly of apatite, and so are your bones. Pale green, blue-green, white or brown.

Baryte
Fairly common, crystals tend to be white, but sometimes tinged yellow, brown or red. Often glassy-looking and clear. Heavy to hold.

Augite
Short, fat column-shaped crystals with eight sides. Black to dark green. Augite is mainly found in basalt and other types of igneous rocks.

Gypsum
Crystals found in prisms, needles or tabular plates. Can be white, but clear pieces were once used as a form of glass. Scratches with fingernail.

Milky quartz
The most common variety of quartz, and easily found. Opaque, white. Found as crystals or small lumps. All quartzes are part of the silicate family.

Mica
Two main types: biotite is black or brown and shiny, and muscovite is white and silvery. Both have thin flakes, and are common in granites.

Talc
The softest mineral, made of silicon, magnesium, oxygen and hydrogen. Pale green, but can be white. Easily crushed, used in talcum powder.

Calcite
Made of calcium, carbon and oxygen. White, but can be green, yellow or blue. Six-sided shapes, forms "fur" inside kettles. Scratches with knife.

Feldspar
Made up of a variety of elements, feldspars are easily found in many igneous rocks. Six-sided crystals, ranging from white to pale pink.

Rock crystal
A type of quartz, clear and transparent. Found as crystals or small lumps. Sometimes mistaken for diamonds. Used to make decorative objects.

Olivine
Made of magnesium, iron, silicon and oxygen. Usually forms grainy masses and often olive green, but some white or black. Weathers to brown.

Hornblende
Consists of many different elements. Large crystals, green or black. Found in a wide range of both igneous and metamorphic rocks, especially amphibolite.

BIRTHSTONES

Some gemstones, known as birthstones, have been dedicated to the months of the years. You can match the month of your birthday to a particular gem.

 January : garnet

 February : amethyst

 March : aquamarine

 April : diamond

 May : emerald

 June : pearl

 July : ruby

 August : peridot

 September : sapphire

 October : opal

 November : topaz

 December : turquoise

Gemstones

Some crystals are especially prized for their sparkling beauty, rarity and value. They are known as precious gemstones. The stars in the mineral family, they're cut and polished to make spectacular jewels for rings, earrings and necklaces.

Some minerals come in different varieties, producing more than one type of gem. Their different shades are caused by metal impurities in the mineral mix.

Top of the rocks

About 20 of the precious gemstones are the most prized of all, because they are the rarest and most beautiful.

At the top of the list is the diamond, with its flashing fire. Other important ones include red ruby and blue sapphire – both varieties of the mineral corundum – and emerald, which is a grass green form of the mineral beryl.

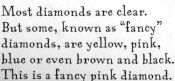

Most diamonds are clear. But some, known as "fancy" diamonds, are yellow, pink, blue or even brown and black. This is a fancy pink diamond.

Aquamarine crystals are named after "sea water" because their shade is a pale blue-green.

A sparkling family

The mineral beryl comes in different varieties, from pink and yellow to green emerald and pale blue aquamarine. The different shades are caused by tiny amounts of chromium in emerald and iron in aquamarine.

Decorative minerals

There are less valuable minerals that are described as semi-precious gemstones. But they can also be very beautiful, and they're easier to find and collect than precious stones.

Semi-precious minerals were first used to make jewels and decorative objects by the ancient Egyptians, Sumerians and Chinese thousands of years ago. Some of the best known are carnelian, turquoise, lapis lazuli and jade.

COLLECTING
Minerals can make a beautiful display.

1. Clean stones in water, using an old toothbrush to remove any mud.

2. Try to identify each one when you've finished cleaning it.

3. Place them in a box with labels and padding to prevent any chipping.

Precious gemstones have always been so expensive to buy that for centuries people have been trying to make copies of them.

Glass and rock crystal were first used, but during the 20th century scientists developed methods of making synthetic rubies, diamonds and other stones. They are still very expensive, and mostly used for industrial purposes.

Precious gemstones to spot

Bright and beautiful, gemstones range from dazzling precious stones, such as diamonds and emeralds, to semi-precious stones such as amethyst and lapis lazuli.

The value of gemstones changes as fashions change. Diamonds and rubies have kept their value for thousands of years. But other stones once considered precious may be less so today. Here are some well-known precious gems.

Spinel
Looking like a ruby, the most prized is blood red. Other shades are pink, blue and yellow. Usually forms as small, eight-sided crystals.

Opal
Made of silicon, oxygen and water. Milky white to a mixture of blue, red and yellow. The most precious is black opal, with more flash and fire.

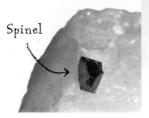
Spinel

Polished opal

LIVING JEWELS

There are other types of precious gems, which come from animals. Red and black coral is highly prized and carved into jewels. Pearls from oysters have been collected for thousands of years – the most valuable are huge pearls from the South Pacific islands.

Ruby
A variety of the mineral corundum. Only red crystals are called rubies. The most expensive shade is called "pigeon's blood" red, found in Myanmar.

Sapphire
Another type of corundum. The most prized is deep blue, but can also be pink or yellow. The most valuable stones are found in Kashmir.

Cut rubies

Pearl

Diamond
The hardest mineral of all, it is made of carbon. Occurs in volcanic kimberlite. Often clear, but also yellow, red, blue, brown, even black.

Cut diamond

Peridot
This is the gem variety of the mineral olivine. Occurs in igneous rocks and ranges from pale to olive green. Very popular in the early 20th century.

Tourmaline
Long crystals with parallel lines along their length. Often black, but blue, green and pink shades also occur, sometimes together.

Emerald
A member of the beryl family, this can be one of the most valuable gemstones. Grass green stones from Colombia are considered the best.

Aquamarine
Another member of the beryl family. Its pale blue-green shade comes from tiny amounts of iron mixed with the mineral. Main source: Brazil.

Imperial topaz
Topaz is usually classed as a semi-precious stone, but the rich golden shade of imperial topaz makes it rare and highly prized. Hard but easily broken.

Cut topaz

Zircon
Sometimes mistaken for diamond. Formed from zirconium silicate, in a range of shades caused by different impurities. Mined in Sri Lanka.

Chrysoberyl
Very hard yellow-green gemstone, exceeded in hardness only by diamond and corundum. A variety called alexandrite changes from green to red in light.

Tanzanite
A blue variety of the mineral zoisite. Crystals are found in gneisses in northern Tanzania. Rich blue, purple and green shades at different angles.

Amethyst crystals

Semi-precious gemstones

You'll probably never be lucky enough to find a precious stone when you're out collecting, but there are lots of semi-precious stones that will look good in your collection.

Good places to search are beaches, where you can sometimes find semi-precious stones in the sand and among other pebbles. Here are some of the best-known examples.

Chalcedony
A member of the quartz family. Fine-grained and doesn't form crystals. It is a porous (absorbent) stone, which means it can be dyed various shades.

Lapis lazuli
Found in Afghanistan and made of minerals including sodalite and calcite. A deep blue, used for thousands of years as a decorative stone.

Smoky quartz
Sometimes known as cairngorm, it forms transparent six-sided crystals. Ranges from a shade of smoky-brown to nearly black.

Amethyst
Another type of quartz, deep purple to pale blue. A popular semi-precious stone used in jewels. Found as crusts lining geodes in volcanic rocks.

Carnelian
A member of the chalcedony family, this ranges from red to brown-red. Has been used to make jewels for thousands of years.

Polished carnelian

Agate
A type of quartz, it is made up of shaded bands. Most agate occurs in rounded lumps. The middle may form a geode with rock crystals inside.

Rhodonite
Bright pink or red caused by manganese, with black flecks and veins. Crystals in tabular plates, found in schists. Used as a decorative stone.

Tiger's-eye
Another member of the chalcedony family. It is composed of tiny fibrous lines that reflect the light, hence its name. Black with gold stripes.

Garnet
A mixture of various elements, it comes in many different varieties. Common dark red to rarer bright green. Found in some metamorphic rocks.

Cut garnet

Topaz
Contains various minerals mixed with water and fluorine. Large crystals ranging from clear to brown, pink and blue. Popular as jewels.

Nephrite
Sometimes called jade, but a different mineral from jadeite. White or green, made of interlocking grains, making it tough. Popular as a carved stone.

Jadeite
A semi-precious stone found as pebbles or rocks in streams. Shades include milky white, but the most valuable is a bright green highly prized in China.

Turquoise
Made mainly of copper, aluminium (aluminum) and phosphorus. Usually found in hot, dry regions once covered in water. Sky blue to apple green.

Polished turquoise

Minerals and metals

Metals are some of the most important materials we get from inside the Earth. Most metals are found as ores – minerals that contain metal combined with elements such as oxygen or carbon.

Copper and gold were the first metals to be used – about 6,000 years ago – to make tools and jewels. They're easier to work than other metals as they're often found in a pure form, not mixed with other substances.

Iron wasn't used until about 3,000 years later, as a lot of heat is needed to extract it from the ore.

This lump of quartz has veins of pure gold in it. The gold can be easily extracted by crushing and then heating the rock.

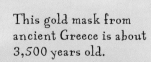

This gold mask from ancient Greece is about 3,500 years old.

Everyday uses

Metals have an amazing range of properties. They are strong and long-lasting and can be beaten into thin flat sheets or drawn out to make wire. Some can be mixed with others to create new metals called alloys.

We have been using metals ever since people first discovered that a glinting piece of copper could be made into a tool. Today, you can find them in practically everything, from aircraft and cars to mobile phones and computers.

Hematite

Chalcopyrite

Galena

Metals in industry

Iron, copper and lead are among the most important metals used in industry today. Hematite is the main mineral ore for iron, while chalcopyrite produces copper and galena is the main ore for lead.

Gold, silver and platinum are precious metals, but they're also important in industry too, especially in the oil refining and electronics industries.

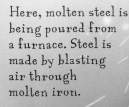

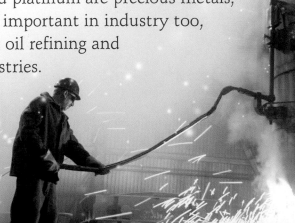

Here, molten steel is being poured from a furnace. Steel is made by blasting air through molten iron.

Ore minerals to spot

The most valuable and useful minerals are the ore minerals. Ores contain metals, such as iron, zinc, lead and copper, which are mined, then crushed and heated (known as smelting) to extract the metals inside. The metals are then refined and processed and used to make all sorts of things that we use every day.

COMMON METALS

Metals are found in many ore minerals, but only about 100 of these are worth the cost of mining them. The most common metals are aluminium (aluminum), iron, potassium, calcium, sodium and magnesium.

Fireworks contain magnesium.

Cinnabar
Red with small crystals. Mostly granular, occurs in sedimentary and volcanic rocks. The source of the fluid metal mercury. Streak: red.

Arsenopyrite
Made of sulphur (sulfur), iron and arsenic. Also called mispickel. Often found with gold and quartz. Streak: black.

Stibnite
Also known as antimonite, the main source of the rare metal antimony. The crystals have a dull shine. Also found with lead and silver. Streak: pale.

Orpiment
This has small crystals, ranging from lemon to orange with a pearly shine. A source of arsenic, once used in yellow paints. Streak: yellow.

Gold
An unmixed element. Found as specks, but sometimes as small lumps called nuggets in igneous and sedimentary rocks. Streak: gold.

Silver
Can be found as small specks and wiry shapes in igneous rocks. Silver-white, but quickly tarnishes (goes black) in air. Streak: silver-white.

Pyrite
Contains iron and sulphur. Known as iron pyrites or fool's gold, due to its appearance. Many fossils contain pyrite. Streak: green-black.

Chalcopyrite
One of the main sources of copper. This mineral is found in igneous and metamorphic rocks. Brass yellow, but tarnishes. Streak: green-black.

Galena
Made of lead and sulphur. Cubic crystals found in sedimentary rocks. When freshly split it is silvery, but tarnishes. Streak: silver-black.

Malachite
Made of copper, carbon, oxygen and hydrogen. Copper produces the light and dark green bands. Used as an ornamental stone. Streak: pale green.

Hematite
Contains iron and oxygen, and found in sedimentary rocks. Also known as kidney ore. Shade from steel to black. Streak: red-brown.

Magnetite
Contains iron and oxygen, like hematite, but in different proportions. Very magnetic, it forms small black crystals. Streak: black.

Sphalerite
Also known as zinc blende, it is the most important source of zinc. It occurs with galena and varies from brown, yellow to black. Streak: brown.

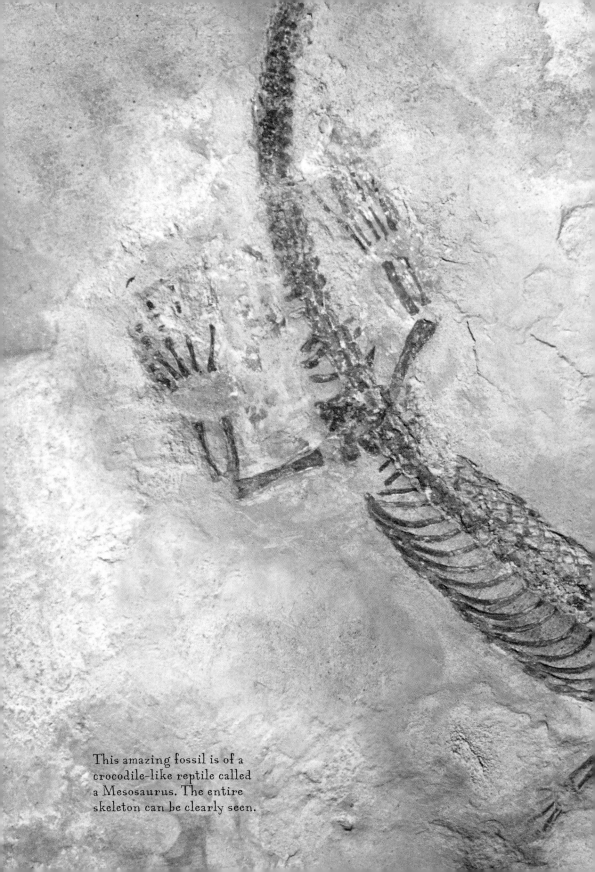

This amazing fossil is of a
crocodile-like reptile called
a Mesosaurus. The entire
skeleton can be clearly seen.

Fossils

Fossils are the preserved remains of animals and plants that lived on Earth a very long time ago.

When you look at a fossil, you are staring directly at a moment in time that has been captured, sometimes hundreds of millions of years ago. Fossils can tell us things about a time when the Earth was completely different, and they can also provide us with glimpses into the future.

FOSSIL TRACES

Sometimes the animal itself isn't preserved as a fossil, but its tracks are.

Fossilized footprints, trails, burrows, borings and droppings that the animal left behind are known as trace fossils.

Hard pieces of an animal or plant do sometimes survive, like the pearly shell of this ammonite fossil.

What are fossils?

If the remains of an animal or plant are buried quickly by sediments such as mud or sand, there is a good chance that they will be fossilized. Then, after thousands of years, a rock hard impression will form, known as a fossil.

Most fossils are found in rocks that once lay beneath the sea, where sediments were laid down all the time. So it's much more common to find fossils of shells and corals than fossils of land animals and birds.

How are fossils formed?

Most fossils are the remains of the hard parts of animals and plants, such as shells, skeletons and wood. The soft parts usually decay, or are eaten, so it's only the remains that are left that are buried under sediment. The sediments press down and harden. At the same time, water washes through the remains, filling up the pores and cavities with minerals and fossilizing them in the rock.

When did this happen?

Thousands, millions and hundreds of millions of years ago. Sedimentary rocks containing fossils were laid down in layers known as strata. The prehistoric period has been divided up into different ages, or eras, named after sets of strata that contain similar fossils.

The oldest fossils ever found are those of simple organisms, such as bacteria and algae, that lived over 3,500 million years ago. Larger organisms, such as trilobites, appeared more recently – 570 million years ago.

Trilobites were small sea creatures with hard, scaly bodies. They can often be found fossilized.

PAST ERAS

*Precambrian – from the birth of our Earth, about 4,600 million years ago.

*Paleozoic – between 570 million and 245 million years ago.

*Mesozoic – between 245 million and 65 million years ago.

*Cenozoic – from 65 million years ago to the present time.

Can we date them?

Scientists use various ways of dating rocks where fossils are found. Some of these are based on something that's very common in the natural world: radioactive decay. Two of these methods – fission-track dating and potassium-argon dating – can record dates going back millions of years. When scientists know the age of the rocks, they can work out the age of any fossils inside them.

OLD BONES

Geologists have used the potassium-argon method to date rocks at sites in East Africa, such as Olduvai Gorge, which contain fossils of early human ancestors.

Fossils come in different types. Look for the following:

Imprint   Cast

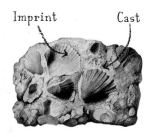

The impression of the outside of a fossil in the rock in which it was formed is called an imprint.

If an imprint is filled with new material, it forms a fossil-like object called a cast.

When a plant or animal is dissolved by water and minerals have replaced the body, it is called a replacement fossil.

This fossil of an ancient fish clearly shows its bony skeleton and spiky tail and fins.

Classifying fossils

Scientists who study fossils are called palaeontologists, and they group fossils in the same way that biologists group living things today – as fish, animals and plants.

Fish fossil   Animal fossil   Plant fossil

Fishy fossils

Some of the oldest and most common fossils are the remains of creatures that lived on the sea bed, where sand and mud settled in layers. This meant their remains were quickly covered and fossilized.

As hard parts are the most easily preserved, sea creatures with shells and some fish with skeletons and thick scales have been found.

Animals and birds

Animals and birds have lived on Earth
for millions of years, but fossils of their
remains are fairly rare. This is because,
although bone is hard, it is easily destroyed
by chemical processes in the soil.

A few complete fossil skeletons of animals
such as dinosaurs have been found, but
mostly in areas that were once covered with
water. It's more common to find fossilized
teeth, because they're much harder-wearing
than bones.

These are fossil
skeletons of sea lizards
called Mosasaurs.

They weren't dinosaurs,
but they lived about 200
million years ago, at the
same time as dinosaurs
roamed the land.

Trees and plants

Fossils of trees and plants are fairly common
because they develop tough trunks and
branches. Fossilized leaves, branches, bark,
seeds, roots and even whole tree trunks
have been found. Some of the oldest known
tree fossils belong to a tree called a Ginkgo
that dates back 245 million years. This type
of tree still grows today.

HUMAN FOOTPRINTS

In 1976, the 4
million year-old
fossil footprints of
two early human
ancestors were
found in Tanzania.
The footprints were
pressed into soft ash,
which hardened and
was covered with
more ash and mud.

Remember that fossils are always found in sedimentary rocks, such as limestone and sandstone. So if you want to find fossils, the best places to look are in areas with these types of rock.

Looking for fossils

Knowing where to look is the most important part of being a fossil hunter. The best way to find out which are the good sites to visit is to talk to someone who knows them and can show you around. Many local geological societies and museums organize trips.

Cliffs and quarries

Riverbanks and cliffs eroded by the sea are good sites for fossil hunters. You can often find fossils in rocks that have fallen down.

Limestone cliffs are some of the best places of all. Rocks exposed on hilltops, in stone quarries and in road and railway cuttings are also good places to look.

Seashells and corals have been found on the tops of hills.

Rock now at the top of a hill may once have been on the ocean floor. The movement of the Earth's plates gradually pushed rocks with fossils up to the top.

Remains of coral in the rock

Fossil shells of sea creatures called ammonites

Sometimes you can find fossils in the most surprising places.

Watery graves

Even areas that are now desert may
contain fossils – if that area was once
covered by water. A good place to look
for fossils is in shale rock formed from sea
mud, and in rocks containing coal that were
laid down in watery places such as lakes,
marshes and river estuaries.

Crinoids, or
sea lilies, lived on
the sea floor about
500 million years ago.

A sticky end

The fossilized resin from pine trees, known
as amber, sometimes contains the remains of
whole insects such as spiders and flies. These
became trapped in the sticky resin and were
preserved and fossilized. Even small animals
such as frogs and lizards have been found
preserved in this way.

This fly got stuck in
pine resin millions of
years ago and the resin
fossilized into amber.

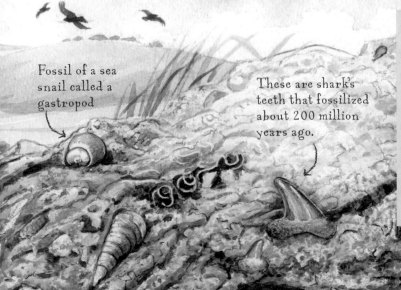

Fossil of a sea
snail called a
gastropod

These are shark's
teeth that fossilized
about 200 million
years ago.

FROZEN IN TIME

The complete bodies
of an ancient type
of elephant called a
mammoth have been
found preserved in
the frozen ground
of Siberia in Russia.
Even the mammoths'
hair and skin
have survived.

Fossil fuels

Fossils can have much more practical uses too.
Most of the fuels we use – in the form of oil,
gas and coal – come from the fossilized
remains of animals and plants. For this
reason, they're sometimes called fossil fuels.

Ancient energy

Coal is formed over millions of years from the
remains of trees and plants that once grew in
freshwater swamps. When they died, layers of
sand and clay gradually settled on top and the
remains were slowly changed by chemical
processes. They were then compressed into
thick, underground layers, or
seams, of hard coal running
between the layers of
sedimentary rock.

Coal

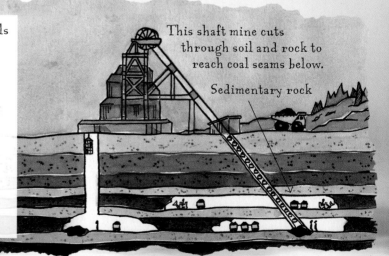

Key to the different levels
in the cutaway picture.

Soil

Compacted peat

Lignite coal
(30% carbon)

Bituminous coal
(60% carbon)

Anthracite coal
(90% carbon)

This shaft mine cuts
through soil and rock to
reach coal seams below.

Sedimentary rock

Oil is formed from the remains of tiny sea creatures, and gas from the remains of land plants as well as sea creatures. These fuels are fluid, rather than solid, and become trapped underground in large pools or reservoirs within the rocks.

Mining and drilling

The coal we use comes from underground mines, or opencast mines (huge open holes dug in the ground).

Oil was first drilled on land, but as more oil is needed so the search for it has also spread into the sea. To extract oil and gas, a drill, supported by a structure called a rig, bores a hole into the ground or seabed.

These are magnified microfossils in rocks. Oil geologists use them to date the rocks.

Oil rig in the North Sea, lying off the coast of Scotland

DIAMOND TIPS

For its size, the most expensive part of a drilling rig is the diamond-tipped "bit". This is used to drill through very hard rocks to reach the reservoirs of oil and gas inside them.

Drill bit

JUST ARRIVED

Humans are relative newcomers on Earth. If you imagine that the Earth is just one year old and was formed on January 1, then humans only appeared at one minute to midnight on December 31.

What fossils can tell us

Most scientists today believe that the Earth was formed about 4,600 million years ago. By studying its rocks and the fossils they contain, we are gradually finding out more about the Earth's history. Even the tiniest remains can reveal the most fascinating information.

Early life

The earliest forms of life were very simple bacteria. Then, about 600 million years ago, more complex animals began to appear on land and there was an explosion of new life.

This process of change is known as evolution. Thousands of plants and animals have become extinct, but we know what they looked like from their fossil remains.

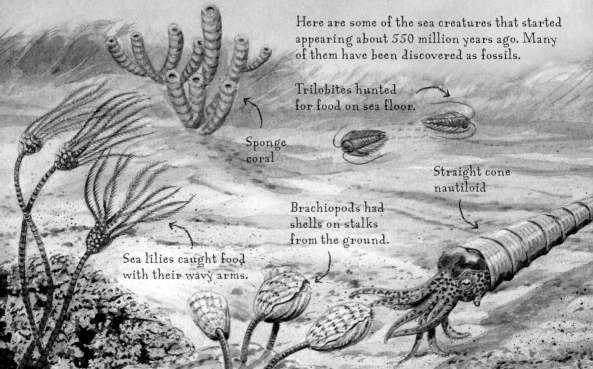

Here are some of the sea creatures that started appearing about 550 million years ago. Many of them have been discovered as fossils.

Trilobites hunted for food on sea floor.

Sponge coral

Straight cone nautiloid

Brachiopods had shells on stalks from the ground.

Sea lilies caught food with their wavy arms.

The oldest fossils

The oldest fossils that have been found all show extremely simple forms of life, such as bacteria and algae. Some of these date back to around 3,500 million years ago. Similar forms of life can still be found today.

Some bacteria fossils, like these, are 3,500 million years old.

Fossil clues

Most fossils show the bones, teeth or shells of prehistoric creatures, and palaeontologists can learn a lot about an animal from these clues.

   For example, the size and width of bones can give an idea of what the creature looked like, its size and weight. The shape of an animal's teeth can indicate the kind of food – whether meat or plants – that it could chew.

This fossil of a Triceratops suggests it snipped leaves with its beak-like mouth.

SURPRISE FIND

Scientists thought the Coelacanth fish had died out 65 million years ago. So they were amazed when a living one was found off South Africa in 1938.

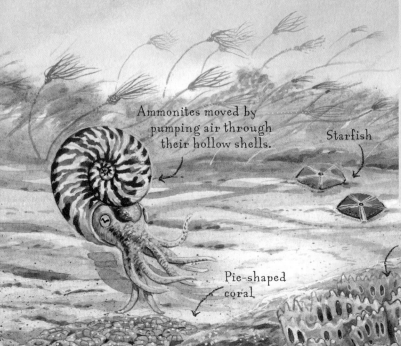

Ammonites moved by pumping air through their hollow shells.

Starfish

Bryozoans formed a lacy network of tiny tubes.

Pie-shaped coral

The world's continents once all fitted together as one giant continent, which scientists call Pangaea. But, over millions of years, this split up into separate pieces and gradually drifted apart.

225 million years ago

135 million years ago

65 million years ago

Today

The past and the future

Fossil remains can also provide glimpses into the future of the Earth. Satellites monitor the Earth's climate all the time, but scientists can only decide if conditions are normal or not by working out what climates were like in the past. Fossils can give them clues about this, and what the future might hold.

Satellite pictures like this one are used to predict rain or droughts across the world. Warm rain clouds are shown in pink.

Drifting apart

Scientists believe that the world's continents were once all joined together. This is because fossils of the same kinds of animals and plants, and from the same period, have been found on both sides of an ocean.

For example, fossils in the Caledonian mountains of northern Europe are identical to ones found in the Appalachian mountains of North America. Africa and North America were also joined together millions of years ago. The fossil remains of Ceratosaurus dinosaurs have been found both in Tendaguru in East Africa and in Utah in North America.

Climate change

The Earth's climate has changed over millions of years.

Plant fossils found in the freezing Arctic and Antarctica, where few plants and animals can live now, show that these areas once had a warm climate and were covered in plants and trees.

Fossil corals can provide clues about sea temperatures millions of years ago, while living corals can tell us about how the climate is changing today.

Seed fern fossil

Horsetail fossil

Club moss fossil

The Arctic region was once covered with lush plants, like this fern fossilized in stone.

The world in the future

With the information they have gathered from fossils and rocks, and using satellites that monitor the movement of the Earth's plates, scientists try to calculate what the world will look like millions of years ahead.

They predict that the Atlantic Ocean will probably keep on opening up, while the Pacific Ocean will close. Australia will continue to move north until it collides with Southeast Asia. China will split in half and mountain ranges will be pushed up all over the world.

MINI MESSAGES
Even fossils of the smallest creatures of all, known as microfossils, can provide vital information to help scientists understand more about what the world's climate used to be like.

Icthyosaur

Fossils from the sea to spot

The most common fossils to find are those of plants and animals that once lived in the sea and other watery areas. Some fossils, such as those of corals and sea urchins, are very common because they have existed for hundreds of millions of years.

Fossils from the sea can be some of the most interesting to collect, because they come in so many different shapes and sizes.

Fossil fish
Fish have hard parts such as skeletons, bony fins and tails and thick scales that are sometimes fossilized. But finding these is quite rare.

Corals
Simple animals with skeletons made of calcite. Fossils often found on their own or in groups called colonies. Oldest are 510 million years old.

Belemnites
Looked a little like modern squids. The fossils are the remains of hard internal parts. Bullet-shaped with pointed end, about 10cm (4in) long.

Crinoids
Also known as sea lilies, because of their long bodies and arms. Common fossils in hard limestones. Related to sea urchins and starfish.

Ammonites
Small sea creatures that used air inside their shells to float. Fossils are flat spirals found in rocks formed 245 to 65 million years ago.

Echinoids
Sea urchin fossils with rounded shells up to 10cm (4in) across. Found in rocks, especially chalk, formed less than 450 million years ago.

Brachiopods
Like bivalves, they have a hinged pair of shells, but a different shape. Fossils in shales, limestones and mudstones less than 550 million years old.

Bivalves
Includes cockles, mussels and razor shells. Their shells are in two parts, which the animals open to feed. Fossils found in shales and limestones.

Trilobites
Creatures with body segments, but only head and tail fossils usually found. In siltstones and mudstones between 550 and 250 million years old.

Trace fossils
A fossil made not from the creature itself, but the tracks of its movements in the sand. These can reveal information about the creature that made them.

Fish teeth
Fossil fish bones are rare but their teeth are quite common. Teeth from rays and sharks have been found in rocks up to 400 million years old.

Gastropods
Commonly known as snails. Shells usually spiral. Fossils found in shales, mudstones and limestones up to 540 million years old.

Starfish
Members of the echinoderm family, which includes crinoids and sea urchins. Found in rocks, such as limestone, up to 500 million years old.

Fossils show us just
how much plants and
animals have changed
over millions of
years. But some of the
earliest plants can
still be found today.

For example,
horsetail grasses date
back 400 million
years, while the
monkey puzzle tree
dates back about 245
million years.

Plant and animal fossils

While the fossils of sea creatures are fairly
easy to find, the fossils of land animals and
birds are less common. This is because their
remains rotted away or were eaten by other
animals long before they could be covered
up and preserved under layers of soil. But
you can sometimes find the fossilized
leaves and other parts of land plants.

Fossil wood
The original wood of
ancient trees turns to
carbon (coal), or may
be replaced by minerals
dissolved in water.
Growth rings can
be preserved.

Whole animals
Whole bodies of animals
have been found
preserved in frozen
ground, and other
animals have been found
preserved
in tar pits.

These fossilized footprints were
made by a dinosaur walking
across mud. The footprints
then hardened and were
covered with more mud.

Leaf

Fossils of leaves of plants and trees have been found dating back hundreds of millions of years. They can tell us much about the climate.

Fossils in fossils

Fossilized tree resin, called amber, has been found with insects and even small animals, such as frogs, trapped inside and fossilized.

Dinosaur fossils

Entire fossil dinosaur skeletons have been found, but these are very rare. Individual fossilized bones are more common.

Plant pollen

Pollen particles from trees and plants can be preserved for thousands of years. They can tell us about the sort of food our ancestors ate.

Plant pollen magnified hundreds of times

Pompeii casts

Victims of the volcanic eruption of Mount Vesuvius were buried by ash. Their bodies decayed, but plaster casts have been made of the spaces left.

FOSSIL TOOLS

The fossil remains of early humans dating back 400,000 years have been found in a cave at Zhoukoudian near Beijing in China.

Scientists have also found some fossils of the tools they made, such as this deer skull cup.

Dinosaur bird

The 150 million-year-old fossil of a dinosaur with feathers was discovered in 1861. It gives clues about the link between dinosaurs and birds.

Human ancestors

The fossil bones of some of our earliest ancestors have been found. Scientists have used them to work out what early people looked like.

This fossilized deer antler was used as a hammer for chipping and shaping rocks.

This is a view of Whitepark
Bay in Northern Ireland,
where the sea is gradually
breaking down the rocks
and cliffs.

Rock collecting

In this section of the book, you'll find helpful information on starting a collection of rocks, minerals or fossils. It shows the kind of equipment you will need on a collecting trip, and how to prepare and take care of your specimens once they're back home.

Starting a collection

Looking for rocks, minerals and fossils can be
great fun, and it's also a good way of learning
about the natural world. But before you go
out collecting, there are some rules you
should always try to follow.

The collectors' code

Always check with the local tourist office
before removing any rocks or fossils,
especially from beaches. Remember that
animals often live underneath rocks, so you
might be disturbing their homes.

Rocks help to keep soil and sand in place,
so only take what you need. If too many
rocks are removed by collectors, beaches
and hillsides can be opened up to erosion
from the sea, wind and rain.

On a beach like this, under chalk
cliffs, you're most likely to find
rounded lumps of flint rocks.

What, when and where?

If you take a notebook and pens, you'll be able to record your discoveries. Try to describe all the material you have collected as clearly as possible, including where you found the samples and the date of discovery.

When you are back home, you can refer back to your notes as you are listing your collection. The more information you have, the clearer the picture you'll be able to build up about the rocks, minerals or fossils in your collection, what they are and where they're from.

CHECK FIRST

There are some places where you aren't allowed to collect. This includes nature reserves, some beaches, and historic sites. You should always check before you go.

Open the day's collecting with details of when and where your expedition took place.

Photos and sketches of the area you visited can help you to identify the rocks you found.

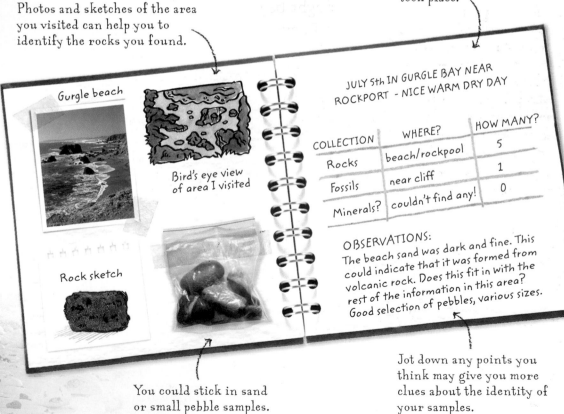

Gurgle beach

Bird's eye view of area I visited

Rock sketch

JULY 5th IN GURGLE BAY NEAR ROCKPORT – NICE WARM DRY DAY

COLLECTION	WHERE?	HOW MANY?
Rocks	beach/rockpool	5
Fossils	near cliff	1
Minerals?	couldn't find any!	0

OBSERVATIONS:
The beach sand was dark and fine. This could indicate that it was formed from volcanic rock. Does this fit in with the rest of the information in this area? Good selection of pebbles, various sizes.

You could stick in sand or small pebble samples.

Jot down any points you think may give you more clues about the identity of your samples.

Preparing your collection

It shouldn't be too difficult to build up a good collection of different stones. On many pebble beaches, for example, you can find hard quartzes, such as flint, chalcedony, agate, rose quartz and smoky quartz. They may look dull and uninteresting when you first pick them up, but there's a lot you can do to bring them to life. This is when some of the most interesting work begins.

Polishing stones

To see the full beauty of your stones and their patterns and shades, it helps to polish and varnish them.

You can polish stones by hand using sandpaper. But, to get the best results, you can use a tumble polisher. This is a machine with a rotating drum in which you place your pebbles, a grinding grit and some water.

This is what some common pebbles look like before and after polishing. You can find these on many beaches.

Amethyst

Green quartz

Red jasper

Polished stones can reveal all sorts of interesting lines and patterns.

On display

You can buy special display cabinets with glass shelves to show off your collection – or you could try making a simple wooden display cabinet yourself.

Fragile, delicate specimens should be wrapped with paper or cotton padding to prevent chipping. If you have a friend who's also a rock collector, you may be able to exchange any duplicates in your collection for other specimens you don't have.

Wooden display cabinet with labelled specimens

If your collection grows to hundreds of specimens, it's important to have a clear recording system – or it can become confusing.

(15) Malachite

Shade : Green
Streak : Pale green
Crystal system: Monoclinic

Found: Cornwall, June 12th 08
Recorded : July 29th 08

CLEANING FOSSILS

CLEANING FOSSILS

When cleaning up your fossils, always chip away from your specimen. In that way, only the unwanted rock will be scratched if your hand slips.

Tap away from the fossil.

Chisel

Collecting fossils

When you are on a fossil hunting expedition, there are two important guidelines to follow.

If you want to remove a fossil from a rock, look closely at the stone to calculate where it will crack. This is so you know the best place to hit it without damaging the fossil.

When you've knocked off the piece of rock with its fossil, wait until you've taken it back home before you chip away at it to tidy it up. Good fossils can be ruined by impatience. Wrap it up in some newspaper to protect it.

Cleaning them

Back home, you'll have plenty of time to work on your new fossil finds. If you can clamp your fossils to a wooden board, it'll make the job of cleaning them much easier.

This ammonite fossil has been tidied up to reveal its patterns. But it has been left on a base of the original rock it was found in.

Making your own fossils

You could make your own fossil imprint and cast. You'll need: a sheet of card, model clay, petroleum jelly, a rolling pin, an object such as a shell or leaf, plaster of Paris, a strip of thin card 5cm (2in) wide and a paperclip.

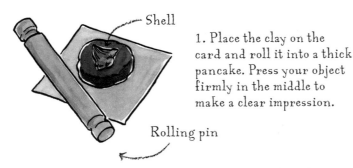

Shell

Rolling pin

1. Place the clay on the card and roll it into a thick pancake. Press your object firmly in the middle to make a clear impression.

1. Paint several layers of latex on your fossil sample, allowing each layer to dry before applying the next.

2. Remove the object and you will be left with its imprint. Now rub petroleum jelly on the surface of the clay.

Petroleum jelly

Plaster of Paris

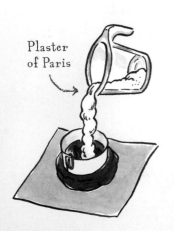

3. Make a collar from the strip of card. Fit it around the imprint, and fasten with paperclip. Mix the plaster of Paris, and pour onto the imprint. Leave it to set hard.

2. When the last layer is dry, slit the back of it with a sharp knife and peel it off the fossil.

Be very careful!

3. Spoon some plaster of Paris into the latex shape until it is full. When set, pop the plaster shape out.

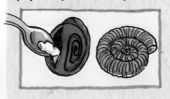

4. Once it has set, after a few hours, remove the collar and pull the plaster away from the clay. You'll be left with an imprint and a cast.

Imprint

Cast

Glossary

Here are some of the words in the book you might not know. Any word in *italics* is defined elsewhere in the glossary.

alloy A mixture of two or more metals, or a metal and a non-metal.

amber A yellow fossil resin from *extinct* coniferous trees.

climate change The change in the world's weather conditions.

continental crust The part of the Earth's *crust* which forms areas of land. It is made mostly of granite rock.

core The central part of the inside of the Earth, which scientists think is made of iron and nickel.

crust The Earth's solid outer layer. It consists of *continental crust* which forms the land, and *oceanic crust* which forms the seabed.

crystal A solid substance, such as quartz, with a regular geometrical shape, in which flat surfaces meet at definite angles.

element A substance that contains only one kind of atom. It cannot be broken down into a simpler form.

era A clearly defined period of time.

extinct An animal or plant species that has died out.

field guide A book for identifying rocks, *minerals* and fossils.

fold mountains A mountain range formed by the Earth's *crust* buckling up into folds when the *plates* of the *crust* push together.

gemstone A decorative *mineral* or organic (living) substance prized for its beauty, rarity and durability.

geode A cavity within a rock that is lined with *crystals*.

geological hammer A hammer specially designed for removing rocks and fossils. It usually has a square head and a chisel edge for splitting rocks.

geology The study of the Earth's rocks and *minerals* and the way they have developed.

glacier A large mass or river of slow-moving ice.

gravel A mixture of rock fragments and pebbles that is coarser than sand.

hot spring A place where hot water, heated by underground rocks, comes to the surface. Also known as a thermal spring.

igneous Igneous rocks are formed when *magma* escapes from inside the Earth, cools and then hardens.

lava Hot *molten magma* that bursts or flows out of *volcanoes* onto the land.

magma Hot, melted rock inside the Earth.

mantle The thick layer of rock under the Earth's *crust*. Some of the rock is solid and some *molten*.

metamorphic Metamorphic rocks are rocks that have been changed by heat or pressure, sometimes both.

meteorite A rock-like object from another planet that has landed on Earth.

microfossil A fossil that is too small to be studied without using a microscope.

These amethyst crystals formed inside a hollow basalt geode.

mineral A non-living substance found in the Earth, such as salt, iron, diamond or quartz. Most rocks are made up of a mixture of minerals.

molten Liquified or melted.

national park A reserve of land, usually owned by a national government, and protected from most human development.

oceanic crust The parts of the Earth's *crust* which form the seabed. Made mostly of basalt rock.

This large group of scallop shells were fossilized in limestone.

oceanic trench A deep trench in the seabed that forms where one *plate* pushes underneath another.

Olduvai Gorge A gorge in Tanzania, East Africa, famous as a site where the fossilized remains of early people have been found.

Pangaea The name given to a huge continent scientists think once existed on Earth. It broke up to form the continents we have today.

plaster of Paris A white powder made from gypsum that sets hard when mixed with water. Used to make sculptures and casts.

plates The separate pieces of *crust* that fit together to cover the Earth.

precious stone A *mineral* of exceptional beauty and rarity often used in jewels.

radioactive decay The process of decay of certain *elements*. As they decay, they give off energy and radiation. The rate of decay can be measured to indicate the age of material such as rock.

sea stack A steep rock in the sea near a coastline. Formed when part of a headland is worn away by the sea.

sedimentary Rock made up of particles of sand, mud and other sediments that have settled on the seabed and been squashed down to form hard rock.

semi-precious stone A *gemstone* that is considered less rare and valuable than a *precious stone*.

smelting The process of extracting a metal from its ore by heating the ore to a high temperature.

stromatolites Simple organisms that have lived from over 3,000 million years ago to the present day.

synthetic gemstone A *gemstone* made artificially by chemical means.

volcano An opening in the Earth's *crust* from which *molten lava*, rock fragments, ash, dust and gases are forced out from below the Earth's surface.

weathering The breakdown of rocks by the action of wind, rain, snow, cold and heat.

Index

Acknowledgements

Every effort has been made to trace the copyright holders of material in this book. If any rights have been omitted, the publishers offer to rectify this in any subsequent editions following notification. The publishers are grateful to the following organizations and individuals for their permission to reproduce material

(t = top, m = middle, b = bottom, l = left, r = right):

Cover © Sinclair Stammers/Science Photo Library; **p1** © nagelestock.com/Alamy; **p2–3** © Gavin Kingcome/Science Photo Library; **p4** © Visuals Unlimited/Corbis; **p6–7** © Phil McDermott/Alamy; **p8–9** © Ashley Cooper/Corbis; **p10** (t) © studiomode/Alamy; **p11** (t) © Elvele Images/Alamy; (b) © Herve Conge ISM/Science Photo Library; **p13** (m) © Martin Land/Science Photo Library; **p20-21** © Douglas Peebles/Corbis; **p22-23** © Mauritius/Superstock; **p24-25** (t) © AM Corporation/Alamy; **p28-29** © Tom Bean/Corbis; **p30** (b) © Peter Horree/Alamy; **p31** (t) © Rough Guides/Alamy; **p33** (bl) © United States Geological Survey; (mr) © Dr Richard Busch; **p34** (b) © DEA/L. Romano/De Agostini Picture Library/Getty Images; **p35** (br) © Andy Sotiriou/Digital Vision/Getty Images; **p36** (b) © David Wall/Alamy; **p37** (bl) © United States Geological Survey; (br) © Dave Dyet; **p38** (b) © Tom Bean/Corbis; **p39** (tr) © AAA Photostock/Alamy; **p40** (bl) © David Ball/Alamy; **p41** (m) © Dave Dyet; **p42** (br) © The Natural History Museum/Alamy; **p43** (b) © Richard Murphy/Alamy; **p44-45** © Dirk Wiersma/Science Photo Library; **p46** (b) © Maurice Nimmo, Frank Lane Picture Agency/Corbis; **p47** (t) © E.R. Degginger/Alamy; (ml) © Steve Hamblin/Alamy; **p48** (b) © Lawrence Lawry/Science Photo Library; **p49** (br) © Kari Marttila/Alamy; **p50** (b) © Sebastien Baussais/Alamy; **p51** (tr) © crystalclassics.co.uk; (bl) © Dave Dyet; **p52** (m) © United States Geological Survey; **p53** (tl, m) © United States Geological Survey; **p54** (l) © JewelryStock/Alamy; (b) © Christies Images/Corbis; **p55** (t) © Wildlife GmbH/Alamy; **p56** (m) © GC Minerals/Alamy; (br) © Photodisc/Alamy; **p57** (tl) © Steve Hamblin/Alamy; (tl) © crystalclassics.co.uk; (tm) © Jewellery Specialist/Alamy; (tr) © crystalclassics.co.uk; (bl) © Jewellery Specialist/Alamy; (bm, br) © The Natural History Museum/Alamy; (mr) © Smithsonian Institution/Corbis; **p59** (tr) © Chris Ralph/Nevada-outback-gems.com; (ml) © The Natural History Museum/Alamy; (mr) © United States Geological Survey; (bl) © Maurice Nimmo, Frank Lane Picture Agency/Corbis; (bm) © Dave Dyet; **p60** (bl) © Layne Kennedy/Corbis; (m) © Peter Horree/Alamy; **p61** (b) © Ria Novosti/Science Photo Library; **p62** (m, bm, br) © United States Geological Survey; **p63** (tl, tr) © United States Geological Survey; **p64-65** © Chris Howes/Wild Places Photography/Alamy; **p68** (b) © David R. Frazier Photolibrary Inc./Alamy; **p69** © Ken Lucas/Ardea.com; **p72** (m) © United States Geological Survey; **p73** (tr) © Darlyne A. Murawski/Still Pictures; (b) © Robert Harding Picture Library/Alamy; **p76** (m) © Digital Vision; **p77** (tr) © ISM/Oxford Scientific; **p80** (bl) © John Cancalosi/naturepl.com; **p82-83** © NTPL/Joe Cornish; **p84** © NTPL/Derek Croucher; **p85** (ml) © Digital Vision; **p87** (t) © VStock/Alamy; **p88** (bl) © blickwinkel/Alamy; **p90-91** © PjrFoto studio/Alamy; **p92-93** © John Cancalosi/Alamy.

With thanks to Mike Freeman
Additional designs by Marc Maynard and Karen Tomlins
Cover design by Joanne Kirkby
Digital manipulation by Keith Furnival

Additional illustrations by John Barber, Joyce Bee, Trevor Boyer, Hilary Burn, Kuo Kang Chen, Aziz Khan, Tim Hayward, Alan Male, Andy Martin, Annabel Milne, David Palmer, Julie Piper, Chris Shields, Peter Stebbing, Phil Weire and others